The ^almost^ instant assembly book 2

12 more complete acts of
worship for primary schools

Sue & Chris Govus

Kevin
Mayhew

First published in 2001 by
KEVIN MAYHEW LTD
Buxhall
Stowmarket
Suffolk IP14 3BW

ISBN 1 84003 731 8
Catalogue No. 1500426

9 8 7 6 5 4 3 2 1 0

Illustrations by Stephen Greenfield
Cover design by Jonathan Stroulger
Edited and typeset by Margaret Lambeth

Printed in Great Britain

Contents

Key to abbreviations of song books cited

CHB – The Children's Hymn Book (Kevin Mayhew)

KS – Kidsource (Kevin Mayhew)

JP – Junior Praise (Marshall Pickering)

CPB – Come and Praise Beginning (BBC)

CCP – The Complete Come and Praise

Introduction and acknowledgements _____

First of all we would like to thank all the teachers and heads who purchased copies of our first *Almost Instant Assembly Book*. They, and the very positive feedback we have received from others who have used the book, really encouraged us to get scribbling and produce another. So here it is – *The Almost Instant Assembly Book 2*. Perhaps this is one sequel that will prove to be even better than the original.

We have kept the structure the same as before so that, almost at the drop of a hat, the book can be picked up from a shelf and used with very little preparation, each 'assembly' being read as written. However, we hope that won't always be the case, and there will be occasions when teachers will be able to bring in some of their own character and personality, thereby adding yet another dimension to these timeless stories.

Our special thanks must go to our illustrator, Stephen Greenfield. His wonderful drawings have inspired us as we have written and we believe they will captivate and delight the children. Please feel free to reproduce these drawings either by photocopying them onto OHP acetates or paper. They can then be used to bring the stories to life. Colour can be added, either by yourself or the children, and they can even be produced *en masse* for classroom follow-up work or friezes. In a similar way, the cue words can be copied and we have found them to be an excellent way of involving and engaging the children in the presentation.

Finally, we would also like to thank our patient, long-suffering friends and co-workers, Glenys Penton and Andrew Harrison, for all the invaluable advice, comments and helpful suggestions they gave us during the writing of this book.

We often hear staff say that they dread having to 'do' assemblies. Our sincere desire is that this book will, in some small way, remove some of the dread and help in the planning, preparation and presentation of your assemblies. Hopefully children and teachers can come together to enjoy, learn from, and perhaps even be challenged by, these 'acts of worship'.

Sue and Chris Govus
Back 2 School Ministries
March 2001

BLONDIN
PUTTING FAITH INTO ACTION _____

Bible Reference   Hebrews 11:1

Aim   • To help children have a better understanding of what it means to have faith and to put it into action.

Introduction   *Call My Bluff* is the name of a popular television programme. It is a quiz show where the people taking part have to decide the correct meaning of a word from the three alternatives they are given. So let's have a go at playing Call My Bluff.

(You may want to bring two or three children out the front to play or use the whole school and count the number of hands raised for each answer, the correct answer is in **BOLD** type).

Picture 1   HYPOCRITE

A   A parasitic bug that lives on a hippopotamus.

B   An insincere person who says one thing but does another.

C   A medical crate or box used for storing hypodermic needles.

Picture 2   FUNAMBULIST

A   The posh name for an entertainer who makes people laugh.

B   A scientist who is an expert in the study of mushrooms and fungi.

C   A tightrope walker.

Picture 3   FAITH

A   A girl's name

B   A religious belief

C   Putting what you believe into action

You may wonder why I chose these three words. Well, sometimes we meet people who appear to be **hypocrites**, they say one thing yet do another. The story we are going to hear is about a very famous **funambulist** who amazed his audiences and challenged their **faith** in his ability to do something extraordinary. During the autumn of 1860 Charles Blondin performed many different death-defying feats on a tightrope. This is an account of just one of them.

Story
It's the 15th of September 1860, and crowds of people have gathered to watch Charles Blondin walk on a tightrope over 300 metres long and suspended 50 metres above Niagara Falls. Imagine you are one of the crowd.

As Blondin takes his first steps, the crowd goes silent. Very slowly and very, very carefully he begins the long and dangerous walk across the tightrope, high above the raging torrent of water that is rushing far below him. Will he lose his balance? Will he slip and fall? One false move will result in almost certain death, but as he safely reaches the far side the crowd go berserk, cheering wildly, shouting and loudly applauding the man who has just cheated death.

Then Blondin shouts out to the crowd, 'Do you believe that I can return across the tightrope carrying someone on my back?'

Confidently and enthusiastically the crowd responds by shouting back in unison, 'Yes, we believe. Yes, we believe, we believe you can do it!'

Then from the platform high above their heads Blondin calls out, 'All right, which one of you will it be? Who's brave enough to get on my back and let me carry them across?'

The crowd are absolutely silent! No one dares to speak or move a muscle just in case it is misinterpreted. Finally, one man breaks the uneasy silence, 'I'll do it,' he says.

The man is Blondin's manager. His name is Henry Colcord. To the utter amazement and admiration of everyone in the crowd he climbs up to where Blondin is standing, bravely jumps onto the funambulist's back, and is carefully carried across the tightrope to the far side.

Application
The crowd said they believed Blondin could walk the tightrope with someone on his back, but when it came to putting their words into action they were silent. Only one man, Henry Colcord, was prepared to act on what he said he believed – that was an example of real faith!

That's the kind of faith that really changes people and motivates them. In the early days of Christianity, it was this real and strong faith that enabled Christians to stand firm even when they were being persecuted. They were even prepared to die in the arena facing lions or gladiators rather than become hypocrites.

Are you prepared to stand up for what you believe in?

Suggested Songs
Be bold, be strong (*KS*, 17)

God has promised (*CCP*, 31)

One more step along the world I go (*KS*, 273)

**Closing
Thoughts/Prayer**

Dear God

Please help us not to be hypocritical but to stand up for what we believe, and help us to put our faith into action.

Amen.

**Possible
Classroom
Follow-up**

- Discuss

    − Is it always easy to put our words into action?

    − Is it possible to believe in someone or something you cannot see?

    − Should we show respect for the faith of others?

- Make a list of people we trust and whose advice we act on. (Doctors, dentists, teachers, parents, etc.)

HYPOCRITE

A A parasitic bug that lives on a hippopotamus.

B An insincere person who says one thing but does another.

C A medical crate or box used for storing hypodermic needles.

Picture 1

FUNAMBULIST

A   The posh name for an entertainer who makes people laugh.

B   A scientist who is an expert in the study of mushrooms and fungi.

C   A tightrope walker.

Picture 2

FAITH

A A girl's name.

B A religious belief.

C Putting what you believe into action.

Picture 3

Picture 4

CHRISTMAS
THE BIRTH OF JESUS CHRIST _____

Bible References   Matthew 1:18-2:12

Luke 2:1-20

Aim   • To think about the meaning of Christmas and reinforce the narrative of the birth of Jesus.

Introduction   Christmas is traditionally a time when people give and receive gifts. At this time of year shops and television promote the latest toys and games. One of the most popular games over recent years has been Trivial Pursuit.

Let's play our own version of that game now.

Bible Story   *NB: Remember to cover the answers up first if using the visuals!*

Picture 1   **Art and Literature**

Who has had more books and paintings based on his life than anyone else?

Answer: Jesus

Picture 2   **History**

What event in history is considered so important that our calendars are based on it?

Answer: The birth of Jesus

Picture 3   **Geography**

In which town, in the country of Israel, did the birth of Jesus take place?

Answer: Bethlehem

Picture 4   **Sport and Leisure**

Mary did not give birth to Jesus in a posh five-star hotel with a swimming pool, sauna and tennis courts. Where was he born?

Answer: A stable

15

Picture 5   **Entertainment**

Who were entertained at an open-air concert by a large choir of angels, announcing the birth of a saviour?

Answer: The shepherds

Picture 6   **Science and Nature**

What new astronomical feature appeared in the night sky and guided the wise men on their long journey to Bethlehem?

Answer: The star

Application

The birth of Jesus is a very important event in the Christian calendar and is still celebrated around the world today. One of the ways it is celebrated is by the giving of gifts. Christians believe that Jesus was a very special gift from God, because of what he was going to do when he grew up.

As you celebrate Christmas and give and receive your gifts, think about what is behind the celebrations: the birth of a baby – a very special gift from God – his own Son.

Suggested Songs

Away in a manger (*CHB*, 245)

See him lying on a bed of straw (*CHB*, 261; *KS*, 291)

Silent night (*CHB*, 262)

Closing Thoughts/Prayer

Dear God

Thank you for sending Jesus, a very special gift.

Help us to remember what we are celebrating as we give and receive our gifts.

Please help us to have a happy and a peaceful Christmas and to make it a special time for others.

Amen.

Possible Classroom Follow-up

- Discuss
  - What is the most precious gift you have given?
  - What is the most precious gift you have received?
  - What made it precious?
- Design and draw a new board game that can be played with family and friends this Christmas.

ART and LITERATURE

Who has had more books
and paintings based on his
life than anyone else?

Jesus

Picture 1

HISTORY

What event in history is considered so important that our calendars are based on it?

The birth of Jesus

Picture 2

In which town, in the country
of Israel, did the birth of
Jesus take place?

Bethlehem

Picture 3

SPORT AND LEISURE

Mary did not give birth
to Jesus in a posh five-star
hotel with a swimming pool,
sauna and tennis courts.

Where was he born?

A stable

Picture 4

Who were entertained at an open-air concert by a large choir of angels, announcing the birth of a saviour?

The shepherds

Picture 5

THE ALMOST INSTANT ASSEMBLY BOOK 2

SCIENCE AND NATURE

What new astronomical feature appeared in the night sky and guided the wise men on their long journey to Bethlehem?

The star

Picture 6

DANIEL
STANDING OUT IN THE CROWD _____

Bible Reference   Daniel 6

Aim   • To demonstrate to the children Daniel's courage in standing up for what he believed to be right.

Introduction   Either — Ask the children to think about the times when they are tempted to follow the crowd, rather than stand up for what they know to be right.

Or — Tell them about a difficult decision that you had to make, that put you at odds with other people and maybe, made you very unpopular.

Bible Story   *(This poem has been written for audience participation — as the appropriate sound effect is shown the children are encouraged to respond. You may find it helpful to have one person read the poem and another responsible for displaying the cue words, either on OHP acetate or paper.)*

King Darius the Mede was a powerful man.

He had a mighty kingdom, but he was in a jam.

Because, you see, his kingdom was really, really large;

he had stacks of advisers and he'd put them in charge.

Yes, the king had advisers and governors galore,

but most were dishonest, and they bent the **(LAW) (COR!)**

They would duck and they would dive, and they would do some dodgy deals;

they were really, really crafty and as slippery as eels.

Now Daniel, he was truthful, more honest than the rest,

and even old King Darius thought Daniel was the best.

For those crooked advisers, this was really bad news.

They didn't like Daniel and they hated his views.

Daniel was a Jew, a prisoner-of-war.

He'd served five kings of Babylon and maybe even more! **(COR!)**

Yes, Daniel, he was different, a very decent man;

that meant the king's advisers had to come up with a plan.

They schemed and they plotted and they finally found a way

when they remembered Daniel prayed three times a day. **(COR!)**

They really disliked Daniel, so they set a cunning trap;

they knew he could be trusted – he would take the rap.

So one day when Daniel was nowhere around

they visited the king, bowing low on the ground.

Grovelling and creeping they suggested a new **(LAW)**

and if anyone broke it – they would hear the lions **(ROAR!)**

The **(LAW)** it was simple – worship Darius alone.

Don't pray to anybody, except the king upon his throne.

For thirty whole days this situation was to last;

the king thought it was great, so the **(LAW)** it got passed.

Anyone disobeying this unchangeable **(LAW)**

would be fed to the lions – and they like their meat raw. **(ROAR!)**

When Daniel heard of this **(LAW)** he did not delay,

he went straight to his room and he started to pray. **(COR!)**

He made no attempt to hide what he was doing,

even though it could lead to his death and his ruin.

He prayed to his God with all of his might

and those wicked advisers had their victim in sight.

He'd been caught in the act of breaking that **(LAW)**

And now Daniel's in trouble, big trouble for sure.

They went to the king without any delay

and told him how Daniel had continued to pray.

The advisers believed they had got Daniel licked,

whilst King Darius realised that he had been tricked.

But the Medes and the Persians – their **(LAW)** can't be changed,

so despite the king's protests – Daniel's death was arranged.

Down to the den, Daniel was taken in irons,

about to be fed to those big, hungry lions. **(ROAR!)**

Realising there was nothing more he could do

Darius shouted to Daniel, 'May your God rescue you!'

So poor Daniel was thrown to those big hairy beasts

who were quite looking forward to this overdue feast. **(ROAR!)**

Meanwhile, at his palace the king couldn't sleep;

he now knew his mistake and it hadn't come cheap.

By the first light of dawn, he rushed down to the den,

rolled away the big stone and called out to his friend,

'Daniel, did God keep you safe from their big hairy paws,

or were you crushed by their teeth and their really sharp claws?'

(ROAR!)

'O King, I am safe,' then came the reply.

'It wasn't God's plan that today I should die.

He shut the lions' mouths; they couldn't open their jaws

(MIAOW) (COR!)

I trusted my God and stayed true to his **(LAW)**'

So Daniel was freed – without even a scratch, **(COR!)**

'cause Daniel's true God, you just cannot match.

Even mighty King Darius had to agree,

and that's what he wrote in his royal decree.

It's in the sixth chapter of Daniel's book.

If you want to know more – go take a look.

I have to admit, it gets a bit gory,

but I'm sure you can guess the end of the story.

The advisers, they'd plotted, they'd messed with the **(LAW)**,

and now it was their turn, to face tooth and claw.

Yes, they were destined for a horrible fate;

they were thrown to the lions – and they all got ate! **(ROAR!)**

Application

The fact that Daniel was so honest and reliable made him a really valued friend to the king, especially as Darius needed someone he could trust to help him rule his country wisely. This was particularly true since so many of the king's other advisers were dishonest and corrupt.

Daniel was placed in a very difficult and dangerous situation as a result of the actions of others and his own beliefs and principles.

- Consider what you might have done if you had been in his position.
- We may not have to face a den of lions, but everyday life can throw up difficult decisions and choices that have to be made. In facing these challenges do we show similar courage to that of Daniel?

Suggested Songs

Be bold, be strong (*KS*, 17)

Daniel was a man of prayer (*JP*, 36)

My God is so big (*KS*, 255)

One more step along the world I go (*CHB*, 166; *KS*, 273)

Closing Thoughts/Prayer

Dear God

Please help us to be honest, trustworthy and reliable like Daniel.

Also help us to have the courage to make the right choices and take the right decisions, even when that might make us unpopular with others.

Amen.

Possible Classroom Follow-up

- Ask the children to talk or write about situations when they are tempted to do things that they know are wrong or simply pressurised into going along with the crowd.
- Encourage the children to think about their consciences and whether or not they determine the choices and decisions they make.
- Discuss with the children current situations that they may be aware of where people are being persecuted for their beliefs.

Law

Cor!

Roar!

Miaow

EASTER
CROSSES, BUNS AND EGGS _____

Bible References   Matthew 26-28

Mark 15-16

Luke 23-24

John 19-20

Aim   To help the children to understand what Christians believe about Easter and the significance of hot cross buns and Easter eggs.

Introduction   Ask the children what they think about and look forward to at Eastertime, e.g. springtime, holidays, chocolate eggs, egg rolling, egg hunts, hot cross buns, special events at church or with their families.

Easter is a special celebration for Christians. It's a time when they especially remember an event that took place in the life of Jesus involving a cross. The cross has become a very special symbol, so we are going to look at some crosses and see what they mean.

Bible Story

Picture 1   A cross like this is sometimes used when we write a letter, or send a card to either members of our family or someone we really like. This cross or several of them at the end of what we have written, means . . .

Picture 2   LOVE

Picture 1   This cross is used when teachers mark your work. Maybe you've had a few of these crosses next to your spellings or even your sums. If, when doing sums you have put '2+2 = 5' you will get this cross (probably in red ink!)

It does not mean your teacher loves you!! It means you got it . . .

Picture 3   WRONG

Picture 1   You may use this cross in an exam where you have lots of different answers to choose from. When you have decided which answer is correct you put a cross next to it. People who are 18 years old and over are allowed to vote for Members of Parliament. They go to a Polling Station, which is often set up in a school or village hall. There they are given a voting paper with different names on it. They show who they are choosing by putting a cross against the name of the person they want to win. So this cross means you have a . . .

Picture 4   CHOICE

Picture 5   Three crosses, each with a different meaning. At Eastertime Christians think about another cross. It's a different shape to the ones we have looked at already, but Christians believe that it is because of these three crosses that the fourth one is needed. The Bible teaches that all people love to make the wrong choice. The word the Bible uses for this is sin.

Picture 6   Sin, which almost always involves being selfish and self-centred, means we fall short of God's standards. It may only be a little word but right at its centre is the letter 'I'

I want to do it my way!!!

I don't care about you!!!

I am much more important than you!!!

Christians believe that the punishment for sin is death and separation from God; but because God loves the world so much, he sent Jesus, his Son, into the world to take that punishment instead of them. He did this by dying on a cross.

Picture 7   It was such a special event in history, that over the years Christians wanted to remember it and chose a Friday during the spring season, calling it God's Friday. This later changed and today we call it Good Friday. Special buns, with crosses on top, were baked and eaten on Good Friday as a reminder of Jesus' death. Today, many people still eat these special buns; they are called Hot Cross Buns. But that's not the end of the story.

Picture 8   Jesus was buried in a tomb, in a cave. When some of his friends went there on the Sunday they were amazed to find the stone, which had been placed in front of the cave, had been rolled away and that the tomb was empty. Later they discovered that Jesus had come back to life!

They saw him, spoke to him, touched him and even had a meal with him – he was not a ghost! The Bible tells us that over 500 people were witnesses to the fact that he had been resurrected (brought back to life).

Throughout history Christians have celebrated the Resurrection of Jesus by giving each other hen's eggs on Easter Sunday, the Sunday immediately after Good Friday. The egg has become a symbol of new life. Just as Jesus broke out of the tomb, so a chick breaks out of the egg.

As the idea caught on, people started to paint or decorate these eggs to make them look more attractive. Nowadays it is far more popular to give and receive chocolate eggs instead of hen's eggs.

Application

I hope you enjoy your Easter holiday! When tucking into your hot cross buns and eggs this Easter, perhaps you'll remember why we have them. They are symbols to remind us that Jesus died on a cross and came back to life again.

Suggested Songs

All in an Easter garden (*CHB*, 7)

Easter time (*CPB*, 55)

Led like a lamb (*JP*, 151)

Closing Thoughts/Prayer

Dear God

Thank you for sending Jesus to die on the cross to take the punishment for everyone's sins.

Please help us to have a happy Easter but also to remember what we are celebrating.

Amen.

Possible Classroom Follow-up

• Blow and decorate a hen's egg

• Make Chocolate Nests.
  (Melt chocolate and stir in shredded wheat. Shape into nests and leave to harden. Decorate with mini eggs).

• Design and make an Easter garden scene

• Discuss – 'What does it mean to make a wrong choice?'

Picture 1

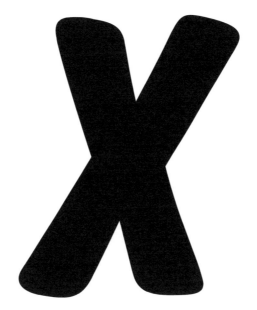

LOVE

Picture 2

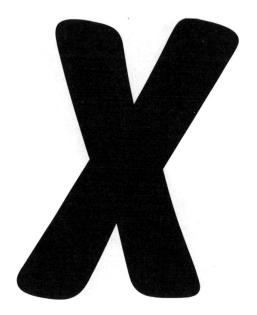

WRONG

Picture 3

CHOICE

Picture 4

X LOVE

X WRONG

X CHOICE

Picture 5

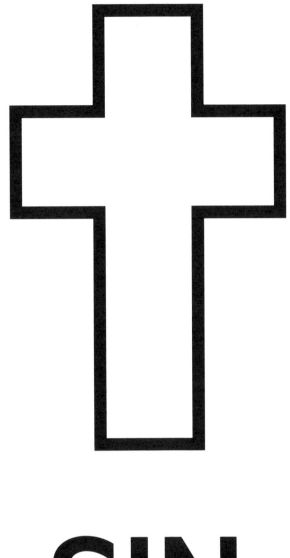

SIN

Picture 6

JESUS

Picture 7

JESUS

Picture 8

JOSEPH
RESOLVING FAMILY CONFLICTS _____

Bible Reference   Genesis 37-47

Aim   To realise the importance of being prepared to forgive and be forgiven.

Introduction   Either – Talk about soap operas

- Who watches a soap opera on TV?

- Who listens to one on the radio?

- What is your favourite soap and why?

- Do you have a favourite character?

- Do they reflect true life?

Or – Relate an incident that happened in your family, where something went wrong and there had to be forgiveness to put the situation right.

Bible Story   Family life is not always easy. It has to be worked at and everyone in the family has to make an effort. Soap operas often try to reflect family life, but these are only made-up stories. Today we are going to hear a true story that really would make a great plot for a soap opera. It begins in the land of Israel (known then as Canaan) and it starts with a dad and his really big family.

Picture 1   Jacob had twelve sons. He also had four wives, but because Rachel was his favourite wife, when her two sons were born (even though they were the youngest in the family) they became Jacob's favourites, especially her first son, Joseph.

This really upset Joseph's ten older brothers, who were very jealous of him. They hated the fact that he was the favourite, especially when Dad spoilt him and gave him special presents like a very expensive coat. When Joseph was about 17 years old he had two very unusual dreams . . .

Picture 2   . . . in one of these dreams he dreamt about sheaves of corn, and in the other he saw the sun, moon and eleven stars. In the dreams the objects were all bowing down and worshipping him. When

Joseph told his brothers about these dreams, he explained that they, his brothers, were the sheaves of corn and the stars who were bowing down. The brothers were furious! Joseph was an arrogant little brat! There was no way they were going to kneel down and worship him! So they began to think of a way to get rid of him.

One day when the ten brothers were out in the fields looking after the sheep, they noticed Joseph coming towards them. This was the opportunity they had been waiting for. They grabbed Joseph, tore off his expensive coat . . .

Picture 3
. . . and threw him into a deep pit. The brothers then sat down to eat a meal and began discussing ways of killing Joseph. In the distance they could see some slave traders on their way to Egypt and this gave the brothers an idea. Why not sell Joseph as a slave? Then they would not feel guilty for killing him, but they could make some money and they would never have to listen to his boasting and bragging again.

Picture 4
The brothers were delighted to receive twenty pieces of silver for Joseph, but how were they going to explain his disappearance to their father, Jacob? They eventually decided to dip Joseph's coat into some goat's blood. When they returned home, the brothers told their father that Joseph had been attacked by a wild animal and killed. Jacob was really upset and mourned for his son.

Joseph, meanwhile, had been taken to Egypt where he was sold as a slave to a man called Potiphar. Joseph proved to be a hard worker and was very loyal to his master. However, things became very difficult as Potiphar's wife really fancied this handsome young slave. Joseph tried to ignore her attentions, but one day things got so out of hand that he ran away. In her anger, Mrs Potiphar went straight to her husband and told him a pack of lies about Joseph. Sadly, Potiphar believed the lies and Joseph was sent to prison, even though he had done nothing wrong.

Picture 5
Whilst he was in the prison, Joseph met up with two other prisoners. They had been servants of Pharaoh, the King of Egypt. Now they were having some strange dreams and told Joseph about them.

The first man had been Pharaoh's wine waiter. He had dreamt about bunches of grapes. Joseph told him that his dream meant he would get his job back. The second man, the Pharaoh's baker, dreamt about baskets of bread, and Joseph told him that his dream meant he was going to die. Three days later the baker was executed and the wine waiter was taken back to work in the palace for the Pharaoh. (This is exactly what Joseph had said would happen.)

The waiter had promised to speak to Pharaoh about getting Joseph released from the prison, but once he got back to the palace, he forgot all about Joseph. It was only when, two years later, Pharaoh had dreams he couldn't understand, that the waiter remembered Joseph.

Picture 6

Joseph was taken out of prison and he listened while the Pharaoh explained his unusual dreams. One of them was about seven fat cows who came out of the River Nile and were grazing on the grass, when suddenly seven thin cows came out of the river and ate the seven fat ones.

Joseph explained to Pharaoh that the seven fat cows meant there would be seven years when there would be plenty of food in Egypt. The crops would grow really well and everyone would have lots to eat. The seven thin cows meant this would be followed by seven years of famine, when no crops would grow and nobody would have any food.

Pharaoh was so pleased with Joseph that he promoted him to second-in-command of the country. He gave Joseph the job of organising the building of big barns, so that extra food could be stored away during the first seven years and brought out to feed the people when the years of famine arrived.

Joseph proved to be a good leader; the dreams came true, and everyone in Egypt had enough to eat during the famine because of Joseph's wise plans.

Meanwhile, in Israel (Canaan) there was also a famine. Along with everyone else Joseph's family were in desperate need of food. Jacob heard there was food in Egypt and he sent his ten oldest sons with money to buy grain.

Picture 7

When the brothers arrived in Egypt they bowed down before the man who was second-in-command, not realising it was their younger brother Joseph. The dreams Joseph had had all those years ago were now coming true. At first he did not let on to his brothers who he was, but tested them to see if their attitude had changed. When he realised that they were sorry for the things they had done in the past, he told them who he was.

The brothers were terrified! What would Joseph do to them now he was so powerful? However, Joseph had learnt the importance of forgiveness and he had all his family move to Egypt.

Picture 8

Jacob was delighted to see Joseph alive, but not only that, all the family were saved from the famine because they were able to settle in Egypt where there was plenty of food for everyone.

Application

In that story we saw a lot of different emotions that are often reflected in family life. There was:

Picture 9

Favouritism	Joseph, Jacob's favourite son
Love	Shown by an expensive coat bought for Joseph
Hatred	Joseph's brothers hating him
Jealousy	The brothers being jealous of Joseph
Violence	The brothers wanting to kill Joseph
Conspiracy	Planning to sell Joseph as a slave
Deceit	Dipping Joseph's coat in goat's blood
Lies	Lying about Joseph's 'death'
Cruelty	Handing Joseph over as a slave
Passion	Potiphar's wife chasing after Joseph
Disgrace	Being put in prison for doing nothing wrong
Isolation	In prison
Ungratefulness	The wine waiter forgetting about Joseph
Terror	The brothers when they found out it was Joseph
Fear	What would Joseph do to them?
Forgiveness	Joseph was prepared to forgive and forget
Peace	Jacob's family was reunited
Joy	They were all saved from the famine

Joseph had learnt how important forgiveness was and because he was prepared to forgive, all the family were reunited and they didn't die from starvation.

You may experience some of these emotions in your family life. Maybe there are times when you get upset and feel jealous or get hurt. Think about whether you make matters worse by your actions, or do you react like Joseph and show forgiveness?

Suggested Songs

He's got the whole world in his hand (*CHB*, 82)

Shalom (*CHB*, 186)

The family of man (*CP*, 69)

Closing Thoughts/Prayer

Dear God

Thank you for our families.

Please help us to be people who are prepared to forgive when we are hurt or upset by others and help them to forgive us.

Amen.

Possible Classroom Follow-up

- Discuss

  - Is it easier to talk to members of our family or our friends?

  - Who do we rely on the most in times of difficulty? (family or friends?)

  - If you were Joseph, would you have wanted to get your own back?

  Look in greater detail at the above list of emotions and actions and think about how they affect our relationships with other people.

- Design

  A coat for Joseph, either by drawing or by using collage.

  The Bible describes Joseph's coat as a richly ornamental long-sleeved robe. It is suggested by some historians that 'richly ornamental' could refer to the expensive threads (gold/silver) or even dyes used to colour the robe, which are thought to have been scarlet, purple and blue.

Picture 1

Picture 2

Picture 3

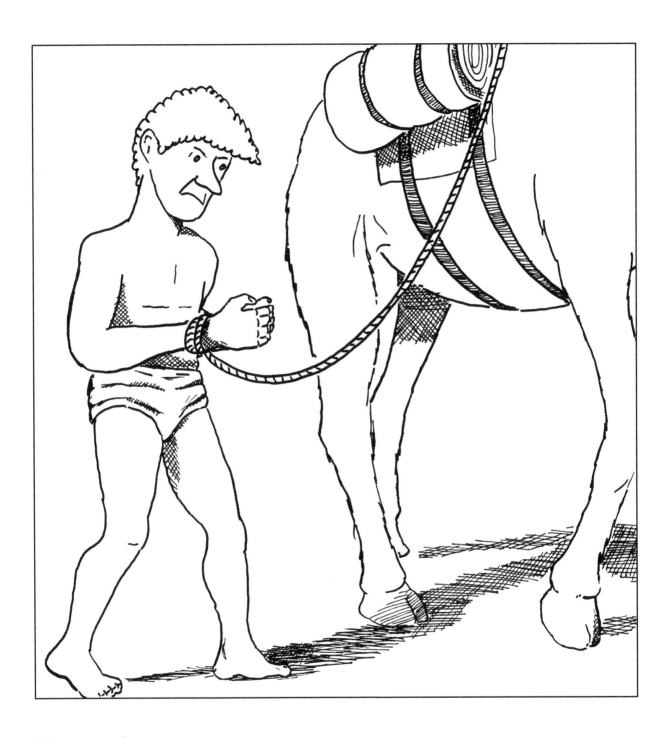

Picture 4

Picture 5

Picture 6

Picture 7

Picture 8

Favouritism	**Passion**
Love	**Disgrace**
Hatred	**Isolation**
Jealousy	**Ungratefulness**
Violence	**Terror**
Conspiracy	**Fear**
Deceit	**Forgiveness**
Lies	**Peace**
Cruelty	**Joy**

Picture 9

LIGHT
SHINING EXAMPLES _____

Bible Reference	Acts 9:1-22

Aim
To think about what it means in a spiritual sense to bring light into the world.

Introduction
Either – Discuss with the children different ways we use light.

– to see by: sunlight, light bulbs, torches, candles, etc.

– for safety: lighthouses, traffic lights, cycle lamps, etc.

– to learn: overhead projectors, television, etc.

Or – Light a candle (it may be helpful to darken the room a little) and talk about how the light from the flame brightens up the area around it, then put a glass over the top and watch it slowly go out.

Bible Story
During our lives we use light in lots of different ways. The story we are going to hear is about a man who saw a very special kind of 'light'.

Picture 1
In the New Testament of the Bible we read about a man called Saul. He was a Pharisee, one of a group of religious people who did not believe Jesus was the Son of God and hated anyone who did. The Pharisees hated Jesus' followers so much that they tried to wipe them out by putting them in prison or even having them killed. We call this persecution.

Saul got to hear that there were many Christians (followers of Jesus) in a city called Damascus. He went to the High Priest and got permission to go to Damascus to arrest and imprison these Christians.

Picture 2
Saul and a group of other men set off for Damascus. As they got near to the city something amazing happened. Suddenly a very bright light from heaven flashed around Saul.

Picture 3
Saul fell to the ground and he heard a voice speaking to him, 'Saul, Saul, why are you persecuting me?'

Totally confused by what had happened and unable to see who was speaking, Saul replied, 'Who are you?'

Again he heard the voice speaking to him, 'I am Jesus, who you are persecuting. Now get up and go into the city, and someone will come and tell you what you need to do.'

Saul stood up and as he opened his eyes he realised . . .

Picture 4
. . . he was totally blind. The men travelling with Saul were speechless and bewildered. They had heard something, but had not seen a thing! Now, realising that Saul was blind, they weren't quite sure what to do, so they led him into the city of Damascus.

Picture 5
They found some lodgings for Saul on Straight Street, at a house which belonged to a man called Judas. For the next three days Saul stayed there thinking over what had happened to him. During that time he did not eat or drink anything and he was still totally blind!

Picture 6
Meanwhile, a man called Ananias, who was one of the Christians in Damascus, had had a dream. In his dream God had told him to go and speak to Saul. He was told he would find Saul in Straight Street, at the house of Judas. Ananias was terrified! He'd heard about Saul and what he was like. He was the man who went around arresting and imprisoning Christians. What would Saul do to him? Even though he was very frightened, Ananias trusted God and so he set off for the house to do as God had told him.

Picture 7
When Ananias arrived at the house he went inside and when he saw Saul he placed his hands on the blind man's eyes. Immediately something that looked like fish scales fell away from Saul's eyes and he was able to see again.

Ananias spoke to Saul about Jesus, explaining how he could be forgiven for all the things he had done in the past and have a fresh start in life. As a result of this, and all the amazing things that had happened to him since he saw the light, Saul was completely changed; he became a Christian – a follower of Jesus.

Picture 8
After this Saul changed his name to Paul. He no longer went around imprisoning and killing Jesus' followers – he had become one of them! Paul spent the rest of his life visiting lots of different countries, where he had many adventures whilst telling other people about Jesus. He also wrote several important letters to groups of Christians and some of these have been included in the New Testament of the Bible.

Application

The Bible describes the world that we live in as sometimes being a dark place where a lot of bad and sad things happen; things like stealing, cheating, fighting and killing. Paul learnt what it was to bring 'light' to his part of the world, showing love, care and compassion, rather than causing pain, hurt and suffering.

The Bible tells us that Jesus described himself as 'The Light of the World' and that he wants us to follow his example. He encourages us to be like him and to be a light to our dark world by being people who bring happiness, joy and peace wherever we go.

NB: It may be appropriate to read the following verses from the Bible to help the children to grasp the concepts being taught here:

Stop oppressing the helpless and stop making false accusations and spreading vicious rumours! Feed the hungry and help those in trouble. Then your light will shine out from the darkness, and the darkness around. You will be as bright as day.

Isaiah 58:9b-10 (NLT)

If you have a fibre-optic lamp, it would make a great visual aid at this point.

Talk about the one light bulb: *Jesus – Light of the world . . .* lighting up all the hundreds of fibre optics [little lights]: *Us – reflecting Jesus.*

Take the fibre optics away from the bulb and there is no light in them – they have no power of their own. *We need to stay close to Jesus and follow his example.*

Replace the fibre optics and they shine for everyone to see: *Lights in our world.*

Suggested Songs

Give me oil in my lamp (*KS*, 66)

Colours of day (*CHB*, 33)

There's a light (*CPB*, 49)

This little light of mine (*CHB*, 212; *KS*, 343)

Closing Thoughts/Prayer

Dear God

Please help us to be the sort of people who bring 'light' into our world.

Help us to be more caring, kind and considerate
and by our words and actions make this dark world a much better, safer place to live in.

Amen.

Possible Classroom Follow-up

- Discuss

  – How many uses for light can you think of?

  – How can we bring 'light' (make a difference) in our part of the world?

  – Who do you know that brings 'light' into our world?

- Search for the places listed below. Christians living in these towns and cities all received letters from Paul. See if you can find them on a map or atlas?

  You may need to use the maps in the back of a Bible.

  ROME

  CORINTH

  GALATIA

  EPHESUS

  PHILIPPI

  COLOSSAE

  THESSALONICA

- Construct a circuit board that 'lights' up!

Picture 1

Picture 2

Picture 3

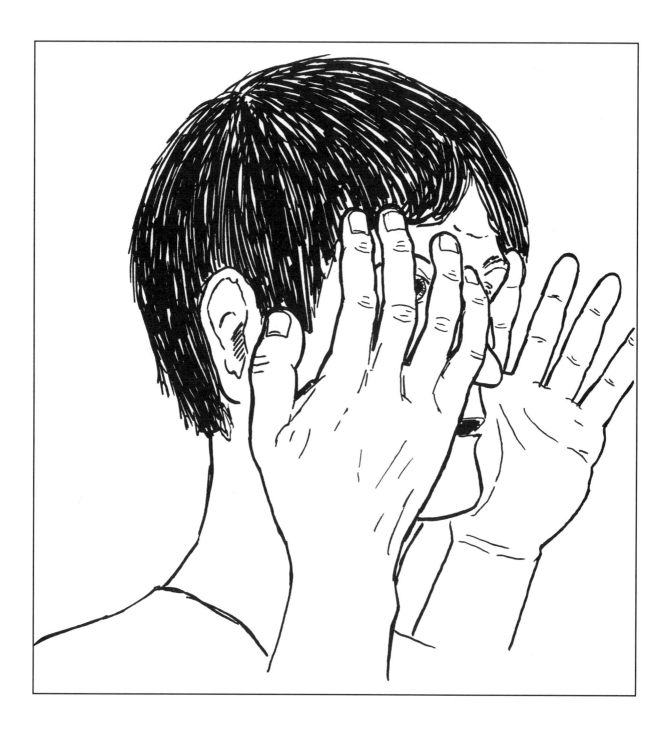

Picture 4

Picture 5

Picture 6

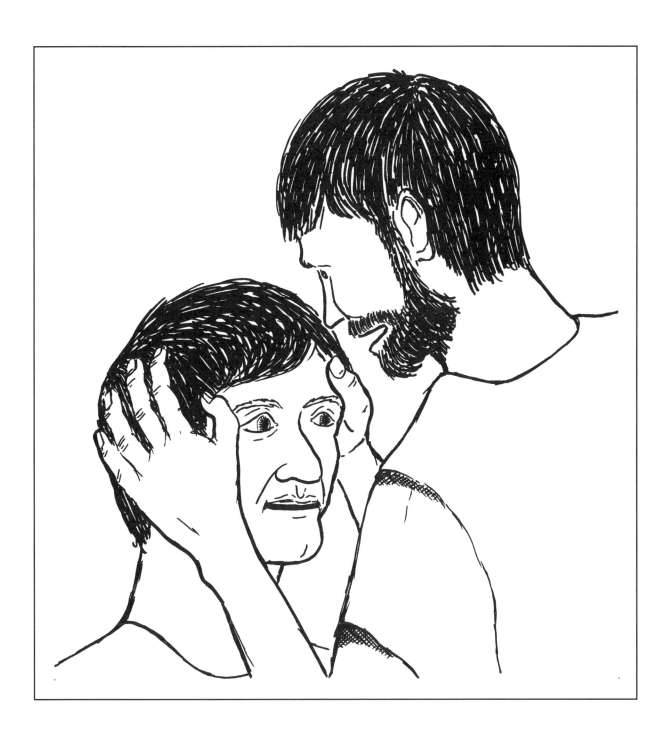

Picture 7

Picture 8

LOVE
WHAT IS LOVE? _____

Bible Reference   1 Corinthians 13:4-8a

Aim   To investigate the word 'love' and try to understand its different meanings. Also, to try and grasp what Christians mean when they talk about God's love.

Introduction   Either – Play a recording of a song about love (possibly a current pop song),

Or – Discuss some of the people and things that we love, i.e. parents, eating ice cream, playing football, watching TV.

Today we use the English word 'love' in lots of different ways and situations but . . .

Bible Story   The New Testament of the Bible was written mainly in Greek. The Greek language at that time was very expressive and instead of one word for love, the Greeks had four words to explain the different kinds of love. Let's have a look at these four words and see what the differences are:

Picture 1   EROS

This is a very special kind of love. *Eros* is the love that a man and woman have for each other, that leads to a very special relationship and often marriage. This love is especially celebrated on Valentine's Day when couples who are romantically attracted to each other often send their partner chocolates, cards or flowers!

Picture 2   STORGE

This is the word that the Greeks used to express the love and affection that parents have for their children and children have for their parents. It can also be used to describe the kind of love we have for things that we really like or like to do. For example, I *storge* my cat, I *storge* eating cream cakes, I *storge* playing football.

Picture 3 PHILIA

This is the love you have for a person who is close to you, someone you really get on well with, a person you can share your problems and difficulties with, confide in and talk to – a really good friend!

Picture 4 AGAPE

This is the word that we find in the Bible, the word that the first Christians used to describe the kind of love that God has for everyone. It's an unconditional love, a love that demands nothing in return.

Christians today believe this means that God still loves us, even if we choose to ignore God or don't believe that he exists. They also believe that Jesus was showing this 'agape' love for the world when he died on a cross 2000 years ago.

One of the early Christians that we read about in the Bible was a man called Paul. In fact he wrote a large part of the New Testament. In one of his letters Paul writes a brilliant definition of *Agape* love. He explains it like this . . .

Picture 5 1 Corinthians 13:4-8a
You may want to read this aloud or have the children read it with you.

Application When God wanted people to know how much he loved them he didn't send them a card, a bunch of flowers or even a box of chocolates. He didn't even offer them his last Rolo. Christians believe he gave us something far more precious than any of these things – he gave us his only Son, Jesus!

Just think for a moment how much better the world would be if everyone showed *Agape* love.

Suggested Songs Jesus' love is very wonderful (*CHB*, 123; *KS*, 208)

Love is something (*CPB*, 16)

Love will never come to an end (*CCP*, 99)

Closing Thoughts/Prayer Dear God

Thank you for loving not just us, but the whole world in a very special way.

Please help us to show that same *Agape* love to each other, so that we can be more patient, kind and caring.

Amen.

Possible Classroom Follow-up

- Discuss

  – How do we show people that we love them? (Family, friends, classmates.)

  – In what ways could *Agape* love be better shown in the school, classroom, home, and world.

- Design and make a card or write a letter to someone you love, thanking them for being there for you.

Picture 1

STORGE

Picture 2

Picture 3

Picture 4

Love is patient, love is kind.
It does not envy, it does not boast,
it is not proud.
It is not rude, it is not self-seeking,
it is not easily angered,
it keeps no record of wrongs.
Love does not delight in evil
but rejoices with the truth.
It always protects, always trusts,
always hopes, always perseveres.
Love never fails.

1 Corinthians, Chapter 13, verses 4-8a (NIV)

Picture 5

NABOTH
GREED AND THE ABUSE OF POWER ___

Bible References
: 1 Kings 21

(1 Kings 22:29-37 and 2 Kings 9:30-37)

Aim
: To help the children realise that when people are greedy and selfish, others can suffer as a consequence.

Introduction
: There are some people in the world who are very good leaders. They may be prime ministers of a government or even the king or queen of a country. They do everything in their power to make sure their people are well looked after and provided for in many different ways.

Sadly, there are also leaders who, when in power, keep the best for themselves and do not seem to care that their people are struggling or even starving to death. They appear more interested in helping themselves to the country's wealth rather than making sure that the country is well run and its people have what they need.

Bible Story
: *(Depending on the age-group of children, you may decide to leave out the part of the storyline that is in italics)*

In the Old Testament of the Bible we read about a very greedy king, who was never satisfied with what he had. His name was Ahab.

Picture 1
: Ahab was king of Israel, which meant he was very rich and had lots of lovely things. He lived in a beautiful ivory palace with loads of servants to wait on him. He had fine clothes, plenty of money and the very best food. He was also married to a very rich and powerful woman – Queen Jezebel. Being the king also meant that Ahab owned lots of land, but even with all of this he was not a happy man. There was something King Ahab wanted and it didn't belong to him.

Picture 2
: Near to the palace there was a vineyard. It was a garden where grapes were growing and it belonged to a man called Naboth. King Ahab wanted this garden. It wasn't that he wanted it for the grapes as he already had lots of other vineyards. King Ahab

wanted this land to grow vegetables. He could imagine all kinds of vegetables growing there for him to eat, and getting this land was very important to him.

Picture 3

King Ahab went to see Naboth and said, 'Let me have your vineyard to use as a vegetable garden, I'll find you another vineyard in exchange or I'll give you some money for it.'

Naboth explained to the king that he wanted to keep the vineyard because it was all that he owned. It was very special to him. This land had been in his family for years. It had belonged to his father and before that his grandfather. He also wanted to pass it on to his sons when he died. He had inherited it and that meant it was against God's law for him to sell it. He did not want to exchange it for another vineyard and he was not prepared to sell it. This made King Ahab very angry.

Picture 4

Without Naboth's consent Ahab couldn't have the vineyard and he went back to his palace in a furious rage. OK, so what if he had gardens and vineyards all over the country – he wanted Naboth's one as well! King Ahab was so annoyed he went to his bedroom, lay down and sulked.

Picture 5

He was so grumpy he wouldn't eat any of the food his servants prepared, he just stayed in his room sulking. Eventually his wife, Queen Jezebel, went in to see him and asked, 'What's the matter with you? Why aren't you eating anything?'

King Ahab explained sullenly, 'I want Naboth's vineyard and he won't let me have it.'

Picture 6

'Are you the king of Israel or not?' replied the queen. 'Get up and eat something and I'll sort this out.' Jezebel left the king and set about writing some letters to the leaders of the city where Naboth lived. She explained that they were to organise a special day of celebration to bring all the people together. She also ordered them to find two people who were prepared to tell lies publicly about Naboth, saying he had cursed God and the king (in those days an act of treason). Jezebel then sealed her letters with the king's seal and sent them off.

The leaders did just as Queen Jezebel commanded. Sadly the people of the city believed the lies being told about Naboth and as a result he was taken and killed.

(Naboth was taken outside the city and stones were thrown at him until he died. Later the wild dogs came and licked up his blood.)

When Queen Jezebel heard that her plan had worked and Naboth was dead, she went back to the king and said to him, 'Go and take possession of that vineyard you want. Naboth's dead, it's all yours.'

Picture 7 Immediately King Ahab went to claim the vineyard; he was absolutely delighted as now he could have his vegetable garden!

Meanwhile, God had told Elijah, a prophet who lived in Israel, what had been going on and instructed him to go to the king. Ahab began mocking Elijah when he first saw him. However, the king began to panic when Elijah confronted him over how he and Jezebel had had an innocent man killed just to get something they wanted.

Picture 8 Elijah explained that not only were they responsible for Naboth`s death but by taking the vineyard for themselves they were robbing Naboth's children of their rightful inheritance and God was going to punish them for this. They were both going to die a horrible death.

(Just as the wild dogs had licked Naboth's blood, so would dogs lick up the blood of Ahab and Jezebel.)

Application Ahab and Jezebel were both very powerful leaders but they abused their position. As a result of their selfish and greedy attitude they were punished, but not before many other people had suffered.

When we act in a greedy or selfish way, it normally results in someone else suffering the consequences of our actions. Before you go to do something that you know to be selfish, stop and think:

- How will this affect other people?

- Will what I am doing hurt or harm someone else?

- If so, what am I going to do about it?

Suggested Songs Kum-ba-ya (*CHB*, 133)

Make me a channel of your peace (*CHB*, 152; *KS*, 248)

When I needed a neighbour (*CHB*, 229)

Closing Thoughts/Prayer Dear God

Please help us not to be like Ahab and Jezebel who were greedy and selfish, only wanting things their way.

Help us to consider other people first, and show us how to share, so that what we do makes the lives of people less fortunate than us better, and not worse.

Amen.

Possible Classroom Follow-up

Discuss

- Ask the children if they consider themselves to be rich or poor.

- Are they happy with everything they have or do they want more?

- Would their views change if they compared their lives to those of children in the developing world?

- In what ways do we sometimes put others at a disadvantage?

- In what ways can we help them?

- If you were in a position of power, what would you change to make life better for others?

Picture 1

Picture 2

Picture 3

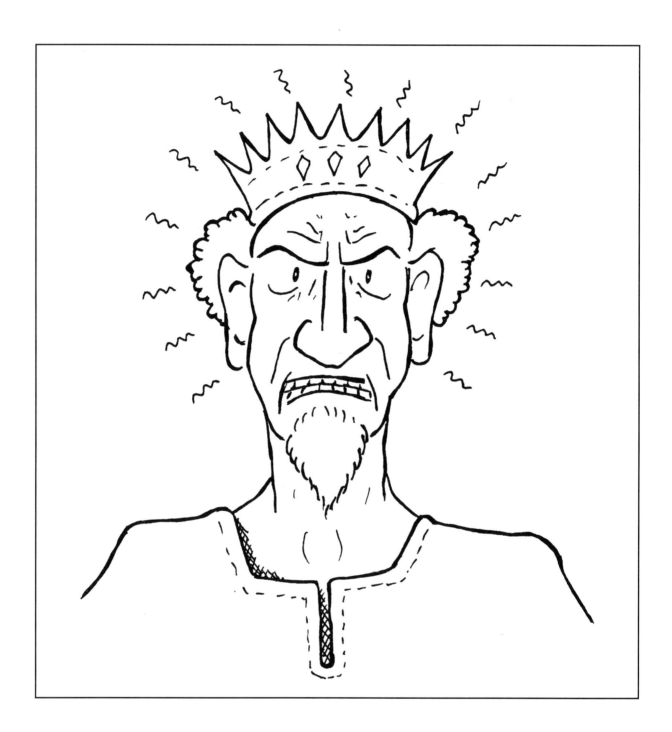

Picture 4

Picture 5

Picture 6

Picture 7

Picture 8

THE PRODIGAL SON
THE IMPORTANCE OF FORGIVENESS __

Bible Reference   Luke 15:11-32

Aim   To demonstrate the important principles of asking for forgiveness and receiving forgiveness from others, based on Jesus' teaching in the Parable of the Prodigal Son.

Introduction   One of the most effective ways that Jesus used to teach people was by using special stories known as parables. These parables can still teach us a great deal today. So although this story is nearly 2000 years old, it has been given a modern setting to help us understand it better.

Bible Story

Picture 1   A very rich man had two sons. They lived in a beautiful house in the country and had everything they needed. The man was kind-hearted and he really loved both of his sons, even though they were very different from each other. The eldest son was very respectable, responsible and worked hard, helping his father to run the family business.

The younger son, on the other hand, was a bit of a rebel. He liked to do things his way and didn't care too much about anybody else. Being rather lazy he didn't do much to help out around the house and not surprisingly there were times when he found it really difficult to get along with his brother and with his dad.

One day the young son decided he just couldn't stay in the house any longer. He wanted to move out and find a flat of his own in the big city. He didn't want to listen to his dad telling him what he could and couldn't do; anyway, it was boring living here in the country. He wanted action, he wanted excitement; he wanted his freedom and independence. However, all of that required money, and lots of it.

Picture 2   So he went to his dad and demanded that his father give him his share of his inheritance there and then. He wasn't going to wait until his father died – that might take years! He wanted the money and he wanted it now! It was his ticket to freedom – he thought.

His father was very sad as he gave his son the money. He knew the boy was making a very big mistake, but there was no point in trying to tell him. It would have just made matters worse, and besides, he wouldn't have listened anyway. The father knew his son would have to learn from his own mistakes, but just as the boy was leaving he said to him, 'I really do love you, Son. Remember, the door is always open, you'll be welcome back any time.'

Picture 3   The last thing on the boy's mind was the thought of ever returning home! He'd set his sights on the big city. Finally he was free! Free to do just what he wanted, when he wanted, how he wanted. At last he could wear all his studs, wear his most outrageous clothes, play his music as loud as he liked, stay out all hours of the day and night. No one was going to tell him what to do any more. Boy, was this going to be fun!

Picture 4   Of course the money helped! It paid the rent on the flat. It really helped to impress the girls – well it paid for the really flash car that impressed the girls. It paid for the gambling and the parties, for the booze and for the fags. For a while the son seemed to be the most popular guy in town. Anybody who was anybody wanted to be seen with him. Sadly what the boy didn't seem to grasp was that it wasn't him that everybody liked . . . it was his money and what it bought.

Of course all this wild living couldn't last for ever, and it didn't. Finally the money ran out, and with it so did all his so-called friends. They just didn't want to know him any more. He lost absolutely everything!

Picture 5   It was a really tough time in the city and lots of people were losing their jobs. When the son had arrived in the city he hadn't bothered to look for work. He was more interested in having a good time. Anyway he had had so much money then, he didn't think he needed a job, but he needed one now! However, try as he might, no one would employ him. It wasn't long before his landlord threw him out of the flat for not paying the rent.

Friendless, jobless, penniless, homeless and hungry, the son was now forced to live on the streets of the big city, just trying to stay alive. To survive he would shelter from the cold in shop doorways and sleep in a big cardboard box under sheets of old newspaper.

Picture 6   As his hunger became more intense, he roamed the streets desperately hunting in the gutters, rummaging through litterbins and dustbins, searching in any place there was the slightest chance of finding a few scraps of discarded food. He was prepared to eat anything! Compared with all of this, life at home with his father and brother had been heaven!

He began to daydream about what life had been like at home. He started to realise how much he had taken for granted, remembering the good times they had spent together as a family. Why had he been so keen to leave? He thought about his luxurious bedroom with its warm comfy bed. He thought about the delicious meals he had enjoyed eating around the big kitchen table. Dad had always made sure there was plenty to eat and loads to choose from. Even the window cleaner and the gardener who came to mow the lawns were always welcome to pop in for a cup of tea or a bite to eat. His dad really was a loving, kind and generous man who had always treated him fairly, giving both him and his brother everything they really needed. It was just that he hadn't realised it at the time.

He began to realise what a big mistake he had made and started to feel very guilty inside. He'd been selfish and self-centred, not caring about anyone other than himself. Then he remembered what his father had said the day he left home, 'I really do love you, Son. The door is always open, you'll be welcome back any time.'

Suddenly, the boy came to his senses. It dawned on him what he needed to do. He would go home and try to speak to his dad, tell him just how sorry he really was and ask for his forgiveness even though he didn't deserve it. Maybe his father would even be prepared to hire him to do a few odd jobs so he could earn some money.

Picture 7 So, swallowing his pride, he left the city behind him and headed for home, wondering anxiously what he was going to say and what sort of welcome was in store for him! He needn't have been so worried. Every day since he had left, his father had been on the lookout for him, hoping and praying that his young son would return home very soon. So, even when the boy was still a long way from the house his dad saw him coming. He instantly recognised him and with great excitement in his heart and tears of joy running down his cheeks, he ran out to greet his long-lost son.

Picture 8 The father was so delighted to see his son again that he threw his arms around him and gave him a great big hug and a kiss. This was despite the fact the boy hadn't had a wash or brushed his teeth for weeks. He was covered in head lice, fleas and smelt like he had been living in a pigsty.

Stumbling over his words and fighting back the tears, the boy began to apologise to his father for the selfish way he had behaved. His dad stopped him. He knew his son and how hard it must have been for him to say sorry. He knew the boy was being sincere. All that was important now was that he had his son back. There would be plenty of time for talking later.

The boy was overwhelmed by his father's love for him and his ability to forgive him. He also really appreciated the long hot soak in the bath, followed by the change of clothes and the slap-up celebration meal. It was his all-time favourite – roast beef and Yorkshire pudding, followed by a really big banana split.

It was really great to be back! Tonight he would sleep soundly in his luxurious bedroom in his warm comfy bed. Now he knew he was home. Home to stay!

Application

Sometimes we can be thoughtless and say or do something that can really hurt another person. Very often that person is someone close to us, like a member of our family or a friend. It's important that we swallow our pride, admit our mistake, and ask the other person to forgive us; otherwise the situation can easily get out of hand and then it can become very difficult to ever put things right.

When Jesus originally told this parable about 2000 years ago, his intention was to help people to understand how much God loves us and wants to forgive us. Today it can also show us the importance of forgiving others when they hurt us and accepting forgiveness from others.

Suggested Songs

Make me a channel (*CHB*, 152; *KS*, 248)

Peace is flowing (*CHB*, 172)

Peace, perfect peace (*CHB*, 173)

Shalom (*CHB*, 186)

Closing Thoughts/Prayer

Dear God

We admit that there are times we do or say some thoughtless and unkind things that can really hurt other people.

Help us to be prepared to say sorry, please forgive us and help others to forgive us too.

Help us also to be able to forgive others when they hurt us.

Amen.

Possible Classroom Follow-up

Discuss

'A home is more than having a roof over one's head.'
(Quoted in the Church of England's report *Faith in the City*)

- Why do many young people argue with their parents and decide to leave home?
- Imagine you are the father in this story. How would you have felt:
  - When the son left home?
  - When the son returned home?

Write a poem either about the things you really appreciate in your home, or about how tough life would be living on the streets.

Picture 1

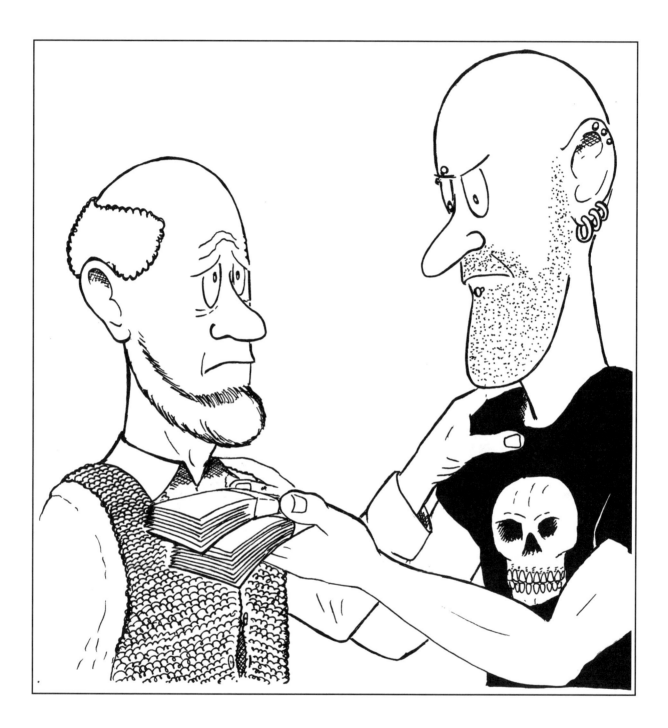

Picture 2

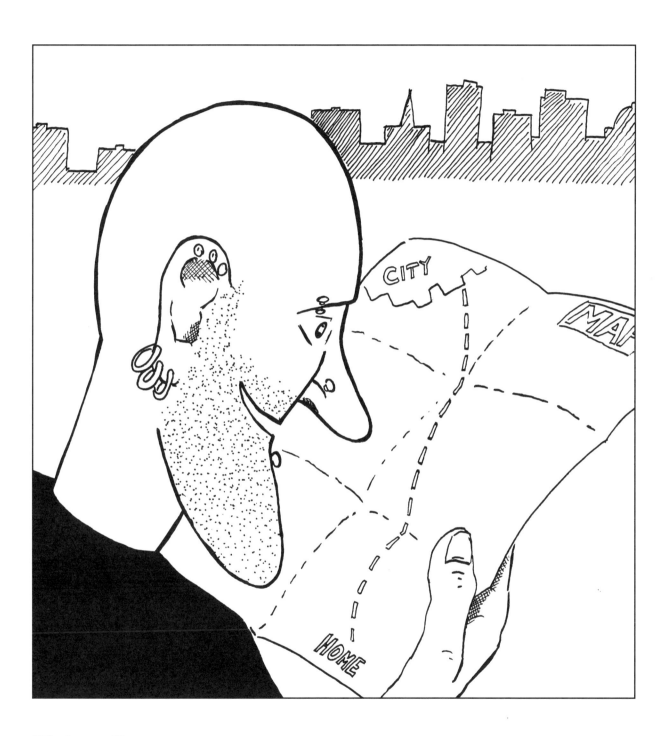

Picture 3

Picture 4

Picture 5

Picture 6

Picture 7

Picture 8

WATER
H$_2$O FOR LIFE! _____

Bible Reference 2 Chronicles 32:1-23

Aim To think about the importance of water and how fortunate we are in this country that it is so readily available to us.

Introduction Who got up this morning, went into the bathroom and had a wash before coming to school?

Who brushed their teeth?

How many of you flushed the toilet?

Who boiled the kettle for a cup of tea?

All these actions involve the use of water and we are so fortunate in this country, because all we need to do is go to a tap, turn it on and out comes clean water.

In Jerusalem around 700 BC, getting clean water wasn't that simple. People had to walk to the nearest well (a hole dug deep in the ground) or cistern (a reservoir dug out of earth or rock where rainwater collected) to get their water. Usually this wasn't a problem, but . . .

Bible Story . . . their king, Hezekiah, was worried. He had heard that a big and powerful army from Assyria, under the leadership of King Sennacherib, was slowly moving down the land of Israel determined to capture and conquer as many cities as possible, including Jerusalem. King Hezekiah got his people busy repairing and building up the walls around the city of Jerusalem to keep them safe. The problem was that the water supply for the city was outside these walls.

A plan was needed if the people inside the city were to survive. King Hezekiah had an idea. Why not dig an underground tunnel from inside the city, going under the walls and out to the fresh water spring? The people worked hard on the project, furiously cutting through the rock with pickaxes; they started at both ends and finally they met in the middle and then the 620-metre tunnel was complete. Then they disguised the area where the tunnel connected to the spring, so that the Assyrian army would not be able to find it. They also blocked up all the wells and cisterns outside the city so that King Sennacherib's soldiers would not have any water to drink.

Even after making all these important preparations, they were still very scared. King Hezekiah encouraged his people, reminding them that even though it was a big powerful army that was coming to attack, they had God on their side and he would help them.

King Sennacherib and his army arrived at Jerusalem and completely surrounded the walls of the city. This was often done by ancient armies and is known as besieging a city. Sennacherib started to boast that he had King Hezekiah trapped in Jerusalem, just like a bird trapped in a cage. The Assyrian army camped around the walls, waiting for King Hezekiah and his people to surrender – after all, it wouldn't be long before they ran out of water in the city . . . or so they thought.

In the city of Jerusalem the tunnel was working well and people were able to get supplies of fresh water; they didn't need to surrender!

Outside the city, the Assyrians couldn't find much water to drink because of the blocked up wells. King Sennacherib was getting desperate and he started swearing and insulting God. He shouted up to the people on the walls of the city of Jerusalem, mocking the fact that they were trusting God and King Hezekiah to protect them. He tried everything he could to scare them into giving up without a fight, but it didn't work.

King Hezekiah and the people prayed to God for help and shortly afterwards all the soldiers and officers in the Assyrian army mysteriously began to die. With no troops left to fight for him, King Sennacherib had to pack up and go back home, defeated and in disgrace. Jerusalem and its people were saved.

Application

King Hezekiah led and protected his people by encouraging them to trust God and by his plan to dig the water tunnel. If you visit Jerusalem today you can still see Hezekiah's Tunnel. On days when the water level is low enough, you can even walk through it and see the amazing job the people did in creating the tunnel all those years ago.

Think about this: How many of you would have washed this morning if you first had to collect the water from a spring, a river or a well?

Today in several countries of the world, many people have to travel long distances to collect water because they have no taps in their homes. Once they have the water, they still have to carry it home and a bucket full of water is very heavy.

Let's think for a moment about how much water we use and how many bucketfuls we would need for just one day:

(You may decide to have a 5-litre bucket to demonstrate size and amount, and to encourage the children to calculate how many buckets are required.)

ACTIVITY	AVERAGE WATER CONSUMPTION	NUMBER OF BUCKETS
FILLING A KETTLE	1 LITRE	0.2
WASHING UP	6 LITRES	1.2
FLUSHING A TOILET	10 LITRES	2
HAVING A SHOWER	30 LITRES	6
HAVING A BATH	80 LITRES	16
WASHING MACHINE	100 LITRES	20
AUTOMATIC CAR WASH	436 LITRES	87.2

We use water for so many things and without water to drink we would die very quickly. We really are so fortunate to have clean water available to us. Do we appreciate it or do we take it for granted and sometimes even waste it?

Suggested Songs

Autumn days (*CCP*, 4)

Have you heard the raindrops (*CHB*, 78; *KS*, 99)

He's got the whole world in his hand (*CHB*, 82)

Oh! Oh! Oh! how good is the Lord (*CHB*, 164; *KS*, 266)

Closing Thoughts/Prayer

Dear God

Thank you for water.

Thank you that we are so fortunate in having water supplied directly to our homes.

Please be with those people who struggle each day to find enough clean water to live.

Also help the organisations that are working hard in lots of ways to improve the water supply for these people.

Amen.

Possible Classroom Follow-up

Work out

- How much water you use in a day or week and display your findings on a chart.

Draw

- A map of your area, noting the nearest water supply to you (rivers, lakes, ponds and wells, etc.).

Survey

The school plumbing system!

- How many sinks are there in the school? (taps, drains, toilets)
- Which sinks/taps are used the most?
- Where is the most water wasted?
- In what ways could the school use or waste less water?

WEDDING
GOD WANTS THE BEST FOR US _____

Bible Reference   John 2

Aim   To illustrate to the children that God wants the very best for us.

Introduction   Either – Talk about weddings:

- who's been to a wedding?

- who's been a bridesmaid or a pageboy?

- what do you like about weddings?

- what do you dislike about weddings?

- who's watched a wedding on TV?

Or – Tell the children about a wedding you've attended, especially if something unusual happened!

Bible Story   *NB: You may want to use the words 'Whatever he tells you to do, do it!' to enable the children to interact with you during the story.*

On the day of a wedding, either at the church, the register office, or afterwards at the reception, there are times when things do not go as smoothly as the people involved hoped or planned. Today a wedding celebration usually lasts a few hours, perhaps a whole day, but in Bible times it was not uncommon for the wedding celebrations to go on for days, maybe even a week.

In the New Testament of the Bible we read about a wedding where something did go dramatically wrong at the reception. This wedding took place in a little village called Cana, which was in Galilee. There were many guests there, including Jesus, his mother Mary and some of his disciples.

Everything was going really well until one of the waiters went to get some more wine to serve the guests and discovered it had all gone! They'd drunk the lot! What a disaster! How embarrassing this would be for the bride and groom and their families, because everyone would remember their wedding as the one where the wine ran out. And what about the caterers? Their reputation was at stake! It had been their job to check there was enough of everything, but they'd really underestimated how much the guests were going to drink.

As soon as Mary heard what was going on, she realised her son would be able to help out. So she went over to Jesus and said to him, 'They've run out of wine.' Then, going over to the waiters she pointed out her son and said to them, **'Whatever he tells you to do, do it!'**

Standing nearby were six big stone water pots. They were empty but were each able to hold about 100 litres of water. Jesus said to the waiters, 'Go and fill those pots with water.'

They probably wondered what he was up to, and it was going to be really hard work collecting all that water from the well, but they remembered Mary's instructions to them: **'Whatever he tells you to do, do it!'** And so they did exactly what Jesus told them.

Eventually all the pots were filled to the brim with water. Then Jesus said to one of the waiters, 'Take a cup and fill it with water from one of the six pots and give it to your catering manager to drink.' The waiter was probably a bit concerned about what his boss was going to think being handed a glass of water in the middle of the wedding reception! But once again he remembered Mary's words, **'Whatever he tells you to do, do it!'** And so he did as Jesus asked.

When the catering manager tasted the drink he was amazed. He went straight over to the bridegroom, took him to one side and said, 'Everyone brings out the best wine first and then the cheaper wine after the guests have had too much to drink, but you have saved the best till last.'

The waiters were utterly amazed; the water had changed into wine! And not only that, it was really good stuff! The catering manager was unaware of what the waiters had done, filling up the pots with water from the well, and now he was raving that it was the best wine he had ever tasted. If only he'd known! Wasn't it great that the waiters had listened to Mary and obeyed what she had told them: **'Whatever he tells you to do, do it!'**

Application

There are many people who believe that following Jesus and being a Christian would be boring and prevent them from enjoying life and having fun.

However, this story shows us that far from spoiling the party, Jesus stepped in and prevented it from being a disaster. Not only did he solve their problem by providing them with more wine, he gave them the very, very best!

The Bible teaches that God has a very special plan for each of our lives and wants only the very best for us. (Jeremiah 29:11-12 '. . .

For I know the plans I have for you', declares the Lord, 'plans to prosper you and not to harm you, plans to give you a hope and a future.')

Suggested Songs

My God is so big (*KS*, 255)

Oh! Oh! Oh! how good is the Lord (*CHB*, 164; *KS*, 266)

Who took fish and bread (*JP*, 286)

Closing Thoughts/Prayer

Dear God

Thank you for this story that teaches us that you don't want to spoil our fun or our lives

but that you want to help us to enjoy them to the full and you want us to have the very best.

Amen.

Possible Classroom Follow-up

Draw

A picture of the wedding at Cana. Perhaps you could think of a witty caption to put on it.

Discuss

- Have you ever been to a wedding where something went wrong? (Car broke down, dress needed a safety pin, best man couldn't find the ring, etc.)

- Were you or someone you know able to come to the rescue?

- If you had been one of those waiters, how would you have responded to the things Jesus asked you to do? Would you have listened to Mary and obeyed her instruction: 'Whatever he tells you to do, do it!'?

'WHATEVER HE TELLS YOU TO DO, DO IT!'

ZACCHAEUS
A FRESH START _____

Bible Reference   Luke 19:1-10

Aim   To show the power of God`s love and illustrate how forgiveness can enable us to have a fresh start.

Introduction   Either – Share a personal anecdote about an occasion when you were forgiven and how you felt afterwards.

Or – Ask the children if they have done something recently that really made someone cross with them. Have they done anything to resolve the situation?

Or – Ask the children to consider this: What's more important, what we look like on the outside or what we are like as people on the inside, i.e. the way we behave towards others?

Bible Story   About 2000 years ago in the city of Jericho, there lived a man whose name was Zacchaeus. Now we don't know a great deal about Zacchaeus, but the Bible does tell us that he was a very short man. It also suggests that not many people liked Zacchaeus. **(BOO! HISS!)** The problem was he was a tax collector . . . **(BOO! HISS!)** a tax collector who worked for the Romans and because of this, his fellow Jews would have seen him as a traitor. **(BOO! HISS!)**

As if all of this wasn't bad enough, Zacchaeus was a thief and a cheat **(BOO! HISS!)** He didn't only collect the money that he was supposed to, he took extra money from the people and kept it all for himself. **(BOO! HISS!)** This had made him very rich! Zacchaeus was a greedy, selfish person and he probably didn't have a single friend in the whole town. He would have been very unpopular. **(BOO! HISS!)**

One day a man who was popular arrived in Jericho. His name was Jesus. **(HOORAY!)** Jesus had said and done some amazing things. He had made people who were very ill better; and he had even brought a man called Lazarus back to life. Crowds of very excited people came out to greet him, to find out what he was going to do in Jericho. **(HOORAY!)**

When Zacchaeus (BOO! HISS!) heard all the noise he probably wondered what was going on. When he realised Jesus was in town he wanted to see him for himself but, because he was so short and the crowds were so vast, he just couldn't get to see Jesus. Perhaps he tried jumping in the air, he may even have tried to force his way to the front of the crowd, but no one was going to let this thieving little cheat push past them. (BOO! HISS!)

Then Zacchaeus came up with an idea! He remembered the large sycamore tree that was growing down the road. What if he ran around the back of the crowd as fast as his little legs would carry him and climbed into the branches of the tree? Then he would be able to see over the heads of the crowd and get a really good view of everything that was going on. So that's what he did.

However, when Jesus arrived at the bottom of the tree, Zacchaeus and everyone else in the crowd were in for a real surprise. Jesus stopped and looked up into the branches and said, 'Zacchaeus, come down straightaway. I want to come to your house today and talk to you.'

Immediately Zacchaeus climbed down out of the tree and led Jesus to his house.

Well, can you imagine it? The crowd were furious. (BOO! HISS!) What did Jesus think he was doing? Why was he going to stay at the house of a thief and cheat like Zacchaeus? (BOO! HISS!) Why wasn't he going to one of their homes? They became very, very angry. (BOO! HISS!)

But Jesus still went. We don't know everything that happened at the house because the Bible doesn't tell us. What we do know is this: as a result of Jesus speaking to Zacchaeus and showing this mean, selfish and lonely man that God loved him and was prepared to forgive him, he was completely changed and had a fresh start. (HOORAY!)

How do we know that? Well just listen to what he said and did after that meeting with Jesus.

Zacchaeus said, 'Lord, right now I'm going to give half of everything I own to the poor . . . (HOORAY!) . . . and if I've cheated anybody out of anything I will repay them four times the amount. (HOORAY!) Jesus was really pleased that Zacchaeus had been willing to change, and by the change in his behaviour he showed the crowd it was for real. (HOORAY!)

Application

Jesus showed God's love and compassion to Zacchaeus, even though it resulted in him being severely criticised for doing so.

Zacchaeus was so challenged by the forgiveness that was on offer that he was a changed man and had a completely fresh start in life.

Christians believe that God wants to show his amazing love and ability to forgive everyone, regardless of who they are or what they have done.

Furthermore, this story can teach us that it's not what we look like on the outside that really matters. After all, being very wealthy, Zacchaeus probably had some really great clothes to wear, but that didn't make him a nice guy.

What's *really* important is what we're like as people on the inside and how we behave towards each other.

Suggested Songs

Jesus' love is very wonderful (*CHB*, 123; *KS*, 208)

Nobody liked Zacchaeus (*KS*, 261)

Zacchaeus was a very little man (*CHB*, 243)

Closing Thoughts/Prayer

Dear God

Please help us to forgive others when they say or do things that hurt us.

Also help others to forgive us when we hurt them, so that we can all have a fresh start.

Amen.

Possible Classroom Follow-up

Discuss

- Do we sometimes judge people just by the way they look?

- Are there times when we ignore people because they appear to be different from us? If we took the time to get to know them, do you think our views would change?

- Jesus wasn't afraid to make himself unpopular by befriending the outcast. What about you?

BOO, HISS

HOORAY!